CONTENTS

47

40

Publisher & Editor-in-Chief: **Thomas H. W. Emanuel** • Executive Editor: **Edward R. Ricciuti** • Staff Writer: **Lou Gianfriddo** • Design: **JAT Associates** • Photography Director: **Stephen H. Taylor** • Staff Photographer: **Tom Buchanan** • Production Director: **Alina L. Massaro** • Photo Editor: **Quinn Tinkoff** • Copy Editor: **Midge Bacon** • Puzzles: **Larry Humber** • Special thanks to: **Matt Kornhaas, Debby MacFadden.**

HULK HOGAN
WWF Champion

Welcome, WWF fans. The WWF is here, with you and for you. WWF athletes compete in London and Glasgow, as they do in New York City and Chicago. Have fun!

The year 1991 has been a banner one for the Immortal Hulk Hogan. At *WrestleMania VII*, he captured the WWF Championship Belt for an unprecedented third time by unseating

then-titlist Sgt. Slaughter. Along with his incredible accomplishments inside the squared circle, the Hulkster is also making big waves on the silver screen. He stars in the major motion picture *Suburban Commando*, that opened in August. In *Suburban Commando*, the Hulkster portrays an intergalactic superhero, Shep Ramsey, who fights the forces of evil here on Earth.

Back in the ring, the Hulkster fights the forces of evil every chance he can get. One of his most prominent challengers at this time is still the Sarge, who

is determined to destroy the Hulkster and *Hulkamania* once and for all. Slaughter and his commanding officer, General Adnan, were responsible for setting the Hulkster's face on fire after *WrestleMania*, and the WWF Champion wants a big piece of them. The Hulkster has a lot of support when it comes to his struggle with the Sarge. The champion's allies, who are better known as Hulkamaniacs, say that they are behind the Hulkster now and will continue to be so until the end of time!

ULTIMATE WARRIOR

The Ultimate Warrior has literally done it all since he entered the WWF. Like a distant comet, he has blazed his way to the highest of honors, leaving behind a trail of defeated opponents. He won the Intercontinental Title on two occasions and even held the WWF Title, winning it from the Immortal Hulk Hogan at *WrestleMania VI* and losing it to Sgt. Slaughter at last year's *Royal Rumble* in a match marred by controversy.

Although a loss of this magnitude would have sidelined almost any other athlete, it did nothing to stop the Warrior. At *WrestleMania VII*, he unleashed his rage on the Macho Man Randy Savage in a Career Match. Savage couldn't contain the Warrior's fury and is now enjoying the lifestyle of an early retirement.

Since *WrestleMania VII*, he

has been in a confrontation with the Undertaker, who stuffed him into an airtight coffin. Once again, the Warrior was physically and mentally able to rebound and has said that he will bury the Undertaker the next time they happen to do battle in the ring!

THE BRITISH BULLDOG

The British Bulldog, who's one of the United Kingdom's most famous athletes, is a licensed powerhouse. He proved this to the world when he wrestled the massive Warlord before the largest audience in the history of pay-per-view at *Wrestlemania VII*, which was held at the Los Angeles Sports Arena. It was a seesaw battle all the way. After the two giants exchanged a volley of clothslines and Irish whips, the Bulldog scooped up the 320-pound Warlord over his shoulder and powerslammed him into the canvas to get the duke. "I dedicated that win to my pet bulldog, Winston," the Bulldog says of the *Wrestlemuniu* victory, Winston, of course, is the Bulldog's loyal companion, and the canine, like his master, also enjoys going after the competition.

WrestleMania and More MEGA EVENTS

WWF

The WWF is recognized as a world leader in pay-per-view cable television setting many records for viewing audiences. The premier of WWF pay-per-view events is the classic *Wrestlemania*, beginning as an American tradition and now awaited each spring around the world. This year's *Wrestlemania VII*, originating live from the Los Angeles Sports Arena, witnessed the titanic battle for the WWF Championship, in which Hulk Hogan took the title from Sgt. Slaughter after an all-out war between the

Some of the WWF super-
stars exhibit incredible
feats of athleticism in
these pay-per-view spec-
taculars. For instance, at
last year's SummerSlam,
the Hart Foundation cap-
tured the WWF Tag Team
Title for a second time
before a thrilled international audience.

Hulk Hogan, in his mem-
orable match against
Sgt. Slaughter at Wres-
tleMania VII, won the
WWF Championship for
an unprecedented third
time before the largest
audience in the history
of pay-per-view. Over
the years, the Hulkster
has made WrestleMania
his own event.

The Royal Rumble *is a 30-man battle royal in which the athletes draw numbers 1 to 30 and then come to the ring at two-minute intervals. Friendships and partnerships, if indeed there are any in the WWF, are thrown by the wayside.*

ropes. Fans in the United Kingdom were able to witness *WrestleMania VII* over Sky Television.

A year earlier, the Hulkster had lost the title to the awesome Ultimate Warrior in a match that went down in wrestling history and sealed their admiration of one another. The Warrior, in turn, lost his claim to the championship against Sgt. Slaughter in January at the *Royal Rumble*, another WWF pay-per-view spectacular.

In addition to *WrestleMania* and the *Royal Rumble*, other annual WWF pay-per-view events are *SummerSlam* and the *Survivor Series*, held on Thanksgiving. Each of these events has its unique character. However, they share high excitement and non-stop action, per-formed by athletes who know well that the world is watching. Thus, every man involved is at the highest state of readiness, prepared to go to his limits and beyond to bring home the victory. The *Rumble*, along with other matches, features an incredible battle in which combatants are eliminated by being tossed over the rope. After the first pair of wrestlers enters the ring, others join the fray one at the time, their sequence of entrance chosen by lot. Thus, the last man picked is much fresher than those who enter the ring earlier.

The *Survivor Series* pits teams of wrestlers against each other. As members of a team are eliminated, the remainder must continue the battle, no matter what the numerical odds are against them. It could turn out that one survivor of a team might be facing four on the other. In this, the *Survivor Series* is unique.

Throughout the WWF, wrestlers vie with one another to compete in the major pay-per-view events. The less scrupulous wrestlers sometimes try to eliminate their competition before the events. At the same time, the stars of the WWF try harder than ever to shine in the squared circle so they will be chosen for the spectaculars. This means that arena action in the months and weeks preceding, for instance, *SummerSlam* is bound to be hot, heavy and furious.

WrestleMania marks the end of one WWF year and the start of a new one. *SummerSlam* marks the height of the summer season and the start of the fall. The *Survivor Series* is the autumnal highlight and, at the same time, paves the way for *WrestleMania*. It is not far-fetched to say that what happens at one pay-per-view event may have great impact on the one following.

There are many different ways of looking at the calendar. For the millions upon millions of WWF fans around the world, the WWF's pay-per-view extravaganzas mark the passing of the year. They represent high points in the annual cycle of excitement that occurs every time WWF stars square off against one another in the ring.

The Survivor Series *pits tag teams of four against one another in elimination confrontations. The survivors of each match advance to the Test of Survival, where three wrestlers on one side can face five or more on the other.*

MR. PERFECT
Intercontinental Champion

As his track record indicates, it seems as if the Intercontinental Title belongs to Mr. Perfect. Just look back at his career. He first captured the belt by winning a single elimination Intercontinental Title tournament shortly after *WrestleMania VI*. Perfect, who's one of the most technically endowed athletes ever to compete in the WWF, went on to defend the title against the most gifted superstars he was able to oppose. He continued to do so until *Sum-merSlam 1990*, when in a match against the Texas Tornado, Perfect lost the championship for the first time. This loss, however, only served to infuriate Perfect, and he won back the belt from Tornado in a disputable rematch.

When the WWF Rampage Tour roared through the United Kingdom last spring, fans turned out in droves to get in on the action. The cheers resounded at the Wembley and Docklands arenas in London, Manchester's G-Mex, Brighton Centre, the Point in Dublin, Belfast King's Hall, Glasgow SECC and the NEC Arena in Birmingham.

Among the stars who wowed audiences were WWF Champion Hulk Hogan, Jake "The Snake" Roberts, Rowdy Roddy Piper, the Ultimate Warrior, Hacksaw Jim Duggan, the Undertaker, Earthquake, WWF Intercontinental Champion Mr. Perfect, the Million Dollar Man Ted DiBiase and Manchester's own British Bulldog.

The Bulldog drew special cheers each time he entered the ring. "It was an immense thrill wrestling in front of my hometown fans," says the Bulldog. "They were just wonderful."

Another native son who found that the tour was a trip back to his roots was the

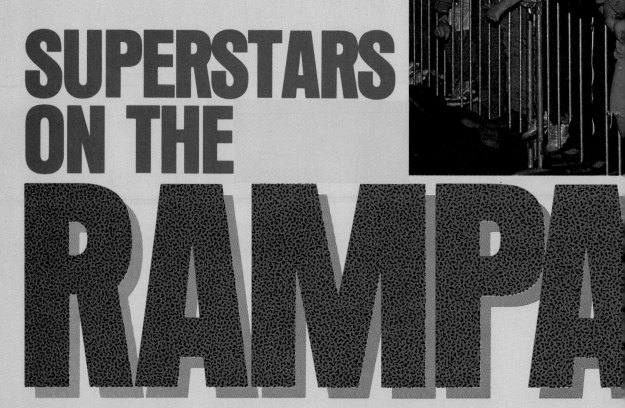

SUPERSTARS ON THE RAMPA

When the WWF blasted through the British Isles, thousands of fans went berserk about all the action, including a match between Scotland's own Roddy Piper and the Million Dollar Man Ted DiBiase.

The wars increased with intensity as the Rampage Tour rumbled onward. The action really ignited when Jake "The Snake" Roberts battled Mr. Perfect for the Intercontinental Championship. Away from the ring and the gym, the British Bulldog relished the opportunity to reacquaint himself with his country. Often he was seen touring various historical and cultural parts of the United Kingdom.

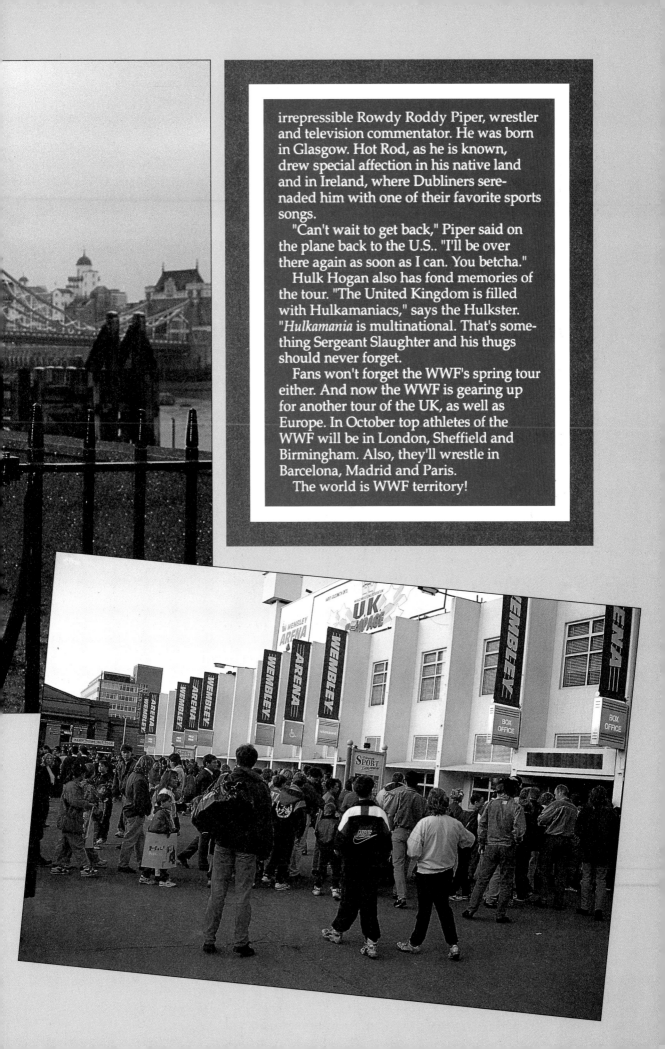

irrepressible Rowdy Roddy Piper, wrestler and television commentator. He was born in Glasgow. Hot Rod, as he is known, drew special affection in his native land and in Ireland, where Dubliners serenaded him with one of their favorite sports songs.

"Can't wait to get back," Piper said on the plane back to the U.S.. "I'll be over there again as soon as I can. You betcha."

Hulk Hogan also has fond memories of the tour. "The United Kingdom is filled with Hulkamaniacs," says the Hulkster. "*Hulkamania* is multinational. That's something Sergeant Slaughter and his thugs should never forget.

Fans won't forget the WWF's spring tour either. And now the WWF is gearing up for another tour of the UK, as well as Europe. In October top athletes of the WWF will be in London, Sheffield and Birmingham. Also, they'll wrestle in Barcelona, Madrid and Paris.

The world is WWF territory!

JAKE "THE SNAKE" ROBERTS

The Snake is one the ring's most cunning superstars. He looks into his opponent's eyes in order to detect any signs of fear. If he happens to notice any, Jake attacks, pounding away with kneelifts and short-arm clotheslines.

Once he establishes his dominance, the Snake pours on the pressure and strikes the adversary with a blazing array of hard-hitting tactics. Then, without warning, the Snake grabs his foe in a front facelock and, with the quickness of a black mamba, drives his foe's head into the canvas. This maneuver is known throughout the world as the DDT, a terrifying move that has rendered scores of opponents unconscious.

However, when Jake pins his foe, the action is just beginning. Seeing his foe in a senseless state, the Snake reaches for his bag and pours Lucifer - his monstrous python - over the defeated soul's body.

THE DRAGON

Former Intercontinental Champion the fire-breathing Dragon returned to the World Wrestling Federation in 1991, and since his comeback, he has really burned up the competition. His wrestling ability can be credited for that.

In the ring, this mysterious athlete blends martial arts and aerial skills with those of scientific wrestling in order to overcome his opponents. His finishing maneuver, the flying bodypress off the top turnbuckle, has been one of the Dragon's best and most successful offensive weapons. Some of the WWF's most dangerous superstars, such as Haku, have fallen victim to this tactic.

The Marvelous, Mischievous Managers

They lurk at ringside. They watch; they think. Often, they interfere in the outcome of a match. They are the managers of WWF superstars. Most, but not all, managers tend to be crafty types, out for the money more than for the welfare of their wrestlers. This type of greed, however, often amounts to success for the wrestlers. Managers who want money will get it only if their wrestlers win. So the managers do all they can to achieve this.

The fortunes of managers vary from time to time. They come and go, but most of the managers in the WWF today have been through the long haul. Here are their profiles.

Jimmy Hart and Paul Bearer.

about him. He gives us the willies. Paul is host of the eerie interview segment *The Funeral Parlor* on WWF Television. He and his Undertaker are a ghoulish duo that threatens everyone in the WWF.

Mr. Fuji

Oriental despot Mr. Fuji is perhaps the most time-tested manager in the WWF. He teaches his wrestlers to inflict pain and torture as a means to winning. True, he lacks a championship among his wrestlers—he's

Mr. Fuji and Slick.

Jimmy "Mouth of the South" Hart

He's a scrawny man, a man who wriggles out of trouble. But he's arguably the top manager in the WWF. A master of distraction, Hart has created major title changes in the WWF. Proof of this is he has a championship team in the Nasty Boys. Never one to rely on one tag team, Hart assembled the Natural Disasters, the largest duo in the WWF. Skinny Jimmy always stays on top.

Paul Bearer

The manager of the fearsome Undertaker, Paul Bearer is a spooky sort. We don't even like to write

had them in the past—but he has come up with formidable men. A relative newcomer, the Berzerker is Fuji's singles entrant. Knowing no pain, no fear, battling out of ruthless instinct, the Berzerker is the kind of man the heartless, innately cruel Fuji can mold into a destruction machine. The Orient Express is Fuji's tag team. This duo shares Fuji's ruthless instincts and suits him quite well, thank you.

Slick
Self-proclaimed the "Doctor of Style" although his

Coach,
General Adnan
and Sensational
Sherri.

garb is rather outlandish, Slick has gained the reputation of being a sleazy sort. He connives and cajoles—anything to get his way. Even so, this beanpole of a man has gathered around him a small but formidable contingent of wrestlers. Like Fuji, he has a top singles competitor and a fine tag team. The former is the massive Warlord; the latter, Power and Glory. Each has taken up Slick's philosophy of winning at any cost, whatever the rules.

Coach

Coach is new to the WWF, but he's already made his mark. Big-time. That's how Coach is. Consider his advice to his former athletes and those he manages now in the WWF.

"Win. Win. Win. Break their legs. Smash their faces. Discipline. Win. Losers are losers. Winners are winners. The only people I want with me are winners."

He's got one. Mr. Perfect, who transferred to Coach when Bobby "The Brain" Heenan opted to forgo his managerial responsibilities for broadcast journalism, signed on with Coach. And, soon after coming to the WWF, Coach showed that he can rival Slick and Fuji in versatility by bringing in the Beverly Brothers, who may make a run at the WWF Tag Team Title.

General Adnan

Acting as the military brains behind Sgt. Slaughter's mercenary band, General Adnan claims that his unconventional mercs have more covert opportunities at their disposal than the Special Forces. As proof, he offers Sgt. Slaughter's fire-bombing of WWF Champion Hulk Hogan. With Slaughter and Colonel Mustafa in his ranks, says Adnan, no one, especially Hulkamaniacs, can be safe.

Sensational Sherri

Sherri is a slinky lady, an incredibly clever manager who always puts her effort into one wrestler. It used to be Macho Man Randy Savage. Typically, when he was down, Sherri turned on him. Now, her man is the Man—the Million Dollar Man Ted DiBiase. Sherri, the consummate vixen, is tailor-made for him. As long as he wins.

THE UNDERTAKER

Coldblooded and relentless, the Undertaker—who's managed by Paul Bearer—is a lethal adversary who seems to be at his happiest when he is burying opponents. The Ultimate Warrior can relate to this because he almost became a cadaver at the hands of the Undertaker. This past spring, as many people are aware, he had an altercation with the Undertaker on Paul Bearer's *Funeral Parlor.*

There, the Undertaker crashed out of a standing casket and attacked the Warrior from behind. A man possessed, the Undertaker battered the Warrior's neck and head with several solid brass urns before locking him in a coffin. After the Undertaker and his

manager left the scene of the crime, a crew of WWF officials, armed with crowbars and electric drills, raced to the coffin and, after a struggle, freed the Warrior. He was barely

breathing and required mouth-to-mouth resuscitation in order to revive.

Next time, says the Undertaker, the Warrior won't be so lucky. He will, adds Bearer, be left to perish.

MILLION DOLLAR MAN TED DIBIASE

The Million Dollar Man Ted DiBiase, the self-proclaimed Million Dollar Champion, is one of the finest technical wrestlers in the WWF—and he's one of the sleaziest. DiBiase firmly believes every man, woman and child has a price, and he often goes to great lengths to prove this outrageous notion.

For instance, during one episode of *WWF Prime Time Wrestling*, the Million Dollar Man selected a youngster from the audience and promised to reward him $100 if he could hold an egg between his chin and his chest for 20 seconds. However, at the 19-second mark, DiBiase broke the egg. To add insult to injury, the Million Dollar Man humiliated the youngster even more by laughing in his face before reiterating the credo that "everybody's got a price."

HOLDS

The holds and finishing tactics that WWF superstars employ are as unique as the individuals themselves. They use maneuvers that are different so that opponents will have difficulty finding a counter and, perhaps most important, holds that best complement their wrestling styles. What's true for the individual competitors is true for tag teams. They too must select maneuvers best-suited to their ways of wrestling.

The maneuvers about which you will read in the following pages are extremely dangerous. WWF superstars are all well-trained professional athletes, and you should not—under any circumstances—attempt to apply these maneuvers yourself.

Some of the superstars in the WWF prefer to use high-impact maneuvers, such as the way WWF Champion Hulk Hogan bounces his foe off the ropes and cuts him

and
FINISHERS

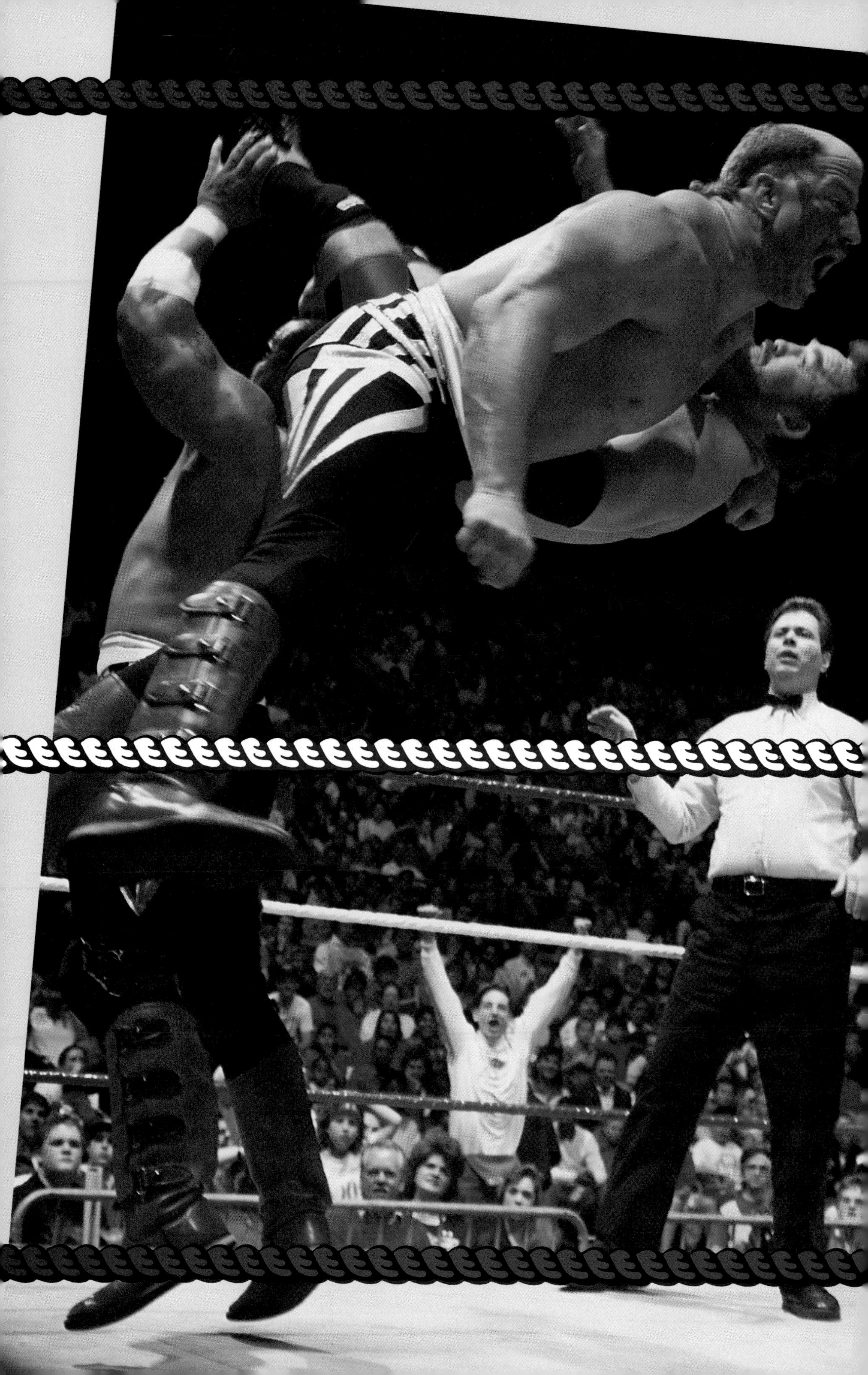

down with a clothesline. The Hulkster fol-follows this up with a crushing bodyslam, which is usually the forerunner to his sig-nature move, the big legdrop off the ropes.

Superfly Jimmy Snuka attacks with a mix-ture of tactics. He uses technical moves, Asian fighting arts, and regularly goes aerial to assault his opponents from above. A tried-and-true veteran, Snuka has the power as well as the agility to use his dazzling mix of attack weapons. His aim is to leave oppo-nents exhausted, mentally and physically, so he can put them to the canvas, then climb to the top rope and launch his amaz-ing finisher, the Superfly Splash. Soaring into the air, he bombs down with shudder-ing impact, then goes for the pin.

The Bushwhackers, Luke and Butch, are deceiving. Their unorthodox tactics, mixing brawling with wrestling maneuvers that never seem to be the same from match to match, confuse opponents. Tough as nails, the Bushwhackers slug away until their op-ponent is set up for the thunderous Bush-whacker battering ram. It's a unique finisher. One Bushwhacker runs the head of the other into the opponent, clobbering him and setting up the pin.

Greg "The Hammer" Valentine, built like a fire hydrant, uses his squat strength to his best advantage, as evidenced by his favorite tactics and finishing hold. His nickname of "Hammer" describes the blow he uses to stun opponents after he has softened them up with a veteran's array of wrestling moves. The Hammer is the elbow with which Val-entine batters down opponents. Once down, they are ripe for the hold that he has per-fected better than anyone else in the WWF, the figure-four leglock. Using his immense leg strength, Valentine applies such pres-sure that a submission is virtually certain.

Hawk and Animal of the Legion of Doom have one of the most spectacular finishing moves in the WWF. It is applied after the opponent is so thoroughly exhausted that he can be lifted up onto Animal's shoulder. Groggy and not knowing what is about to happen, the opponent is a perfect target for Hawk. He mounts the ropes, and then Hawk flies into the air and clotheslines the victim off Animal's shoulders to the mat, where he is pinned.

All WWF stars continually work on the tactics that will bring them victory and glory. They polish and refine, innovate and improvise. If they don't, they will not sur-vive in the squared circle.

HACKSAW JIM DUGGAN

They don't come any tougher than Hacksaw Jim Duggan. When this hard-nosed, red-blooded American patriot sets his feet between the ropes, he's all business. Duggan attacks adversaries head-on and attempts to put them on the deck with big clotheslines and roundhouse blows. From there, Hacksaw pulverizes his opponents with his powerful finishing tactic, the running shoulderblock.

BRET "HIT MAN" HART

Two-time coholder of the WWF Tag Team Title, Bret "Hit Man" Hart has adapted himself remarkably well to the rigors of individual competition in the World Wrestling Federation. In fact, he's so impressive as a singles sensation that at press time he was ranked as one of the leading contenders for the Intercontinental Title, currently held by Mr. Perfect.

One of the weapons in Hart's arsenal is his sharpshooter finishing hold. This modified version of the leg grapevine has now become Bret "Hit Man" Hart's trademark maneuver.

WWF TRIVIA

I t's time for a little WWF Trivia. There are five categories, each made up of three questions.

Award yourself one point for answering the first question in each category, two points for answering the second and three points for the third question, the most difficult.

A perfect score is 30, but consider yourself an expert on the World Wrestling Federation if you get even 25 points. Between 20-25 deserves a pat on the back, too. If you get less than 10, better study up a little.

TOUGH TALK

1 What does everyone have for the Million Dollar Man?
2 Which high-flying two-some parties hard and wrestles harder?
3 Who threatens his opponents with "hard time"?

HISTORY IN THE MAKING

1 Whom did Randy Savage hoist to his shoulder following his loss at *WrestleMania VII*?
2 What was unique about the *WrestleMania VII* bout between Jake "The Snake" Roberts and the Model Rick Martel?
3 *WrestleMania VII* took place at the Los Angeles Sports Arena. What other *WrestleMania* was held there also?

HOMEBOYS

1 Where was Rowdy Roddy Piper born?
2 The Bush-whackers hail from what is-land nation?
3 Hulk Hogan is a native of Ven-ice Beach. In what state is that located.

PHYSICAL ASSETS

1 What WWF superstar has "the largest arms in the world"?
2 Earthquake tips the scales at nearly 400, 430 or 460 pounds?
3 Who won a Super Pose-down at *Royal Rumble '89*?

BRAINS BEHIND THE BRAWN

1 Who manages the Nasty Boys?
2 Who's the "Doctor of Style"?
3 Before signing on with Coach, who managed Mr. Perfect?

SGT. SLAUGHTER

The rules of which Sgt. Slaughter often speaks seem to grow progressively more vicious every time he gets into the ring. By looking back over the past year, one can clearly see just how the Sarge's errant guidelines have affected other people in the WWF.

Take, for instance, *WrestleMania VII*. In his memorable match against the Hulkster, Slaughter went to any extreme to hurt Hulk Hogan. If that wasn't enough brutality for one day, the Sarge, in one of the worst displays of violence in WWF history, then threw fire into Hulk's face during a post-match interview. Hogan isn't the only one who has had to deal with Slaughter's rules. The Sarge has also tortured Hacksaw Duggan in a vicious way. Sgt. Slaughter is definitely one who needs to be put out of commission before he can perpetrate more atrocities of ring warfare.

BIG BOSS MAN

Defender of law and order in the WWF, the Boss Man has had his hands full this past year. At *WrestleMania VII*, he had an Intercontinental Title shot against Mr. Perfect and was on the verge of winning the match. However, Perfect's then-cohorts the Barbarian and Haku ran to the ring and jumped the Boss Man, saving Perfect's title and his hide via a disqualification.

Since then, the Boss Man and the Mountie, who considers himself an "international law enforcer," have locked horns. The Boss Man has vowed that justice will be served, and the Mountie is in for hard time.

THE RIGHT MOVES

Every wrestler has his favorite move.
See if you can match the wrestlers listed with their favorite.

 ◀Legion of Doom

Earthquake▶

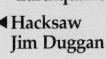 ◀Hacksaw Jim Duggan

Big Boss Man▶

◀Warlord

British Bulldog▶

◀Greg Valentine

Haku▶

 ◀Superfly Jimmy Snuka

Texas Tornado▶

◀The Mountie

Ted DiBiase▶

Spike Slam
Carotid Control Technique
The Claw
Rear Kick
Running Clothesline
Full Nelson
Vertical Splash
Sleeperhold
Figure-Four Leglock
Running Powerslam
Splash From Top Turnbuckle
Doomsday Device

THE MOUNTIE

He calls himself the Mountie and an international law enforcer. Maybe. But his actions in the WWF thus far indicate that he breaks rules rather than enforcing them.

Holds that most lawmen use to bring unruly suspects under control, the Mountie utilizes to inflict pain. Moreover, when he has defeated an opponent, the Mountie hits him with a jolt from a stun gun. The Mountie is as mean as they come. If anybody is guilty of police brutality, it's the Mountie, who is managed by Jimmy "Mouth of the South" Hart.

There is another lawman in the WWF who would like to stop the Mountie's police brutality. He's the Big Boss Man, a rugged former prison guard from Georgia. The Boss Man is determined to end the Mountie's reign of terror.

WORD FIND

H idden in the maze of letters are 12 World Wrestling Federation notables, all of whom appeared at *WrestleMania VII*. They are (in alphabetical order) **BIG BOSS MAN, EARTHQUAKE, HAKU, HULK HOGAN, MR. PERFECT, ROCKERS, SLICK, TED DIBIASE, ULTIMATE WARRIOR,** **UNDERTAKER, VIRGIL** and **WARLORD.** All the names in the word maze read either across or down.

A couple of the names overlap. Take the overlapping letters and unscramble them to answer the following question: *How many times has Hulk Hogan been WWF Champion?* Good luck!

```
V  I  R  G  I  L  O  Y  B  N  Q  F  X  U  U
E  S  P  L  E  G  R  O  C  K  E  R  S  Q  L
C  V  B  U  O  H  X  R  M  L  T  B  E  W  T
S  L  I  C  K  U  D  S  E  V  M  T  W  O  I
G  D  S  P  E  L  U  Z  A  T  R  L  A  C  M
C  T  B  V  O  K  Z  I  Q  T  P  X  R  W  A
A  E  A  R  T  H  Q  U  A  K  E  S  L  C  T
M  D  V  X  Y  O  A  B  G  I  R  U  O  F  E
K  D  N  H  R  G  C  K  U  H  F  P  R  X  W
B  I  R  A  U  A  H  T  Y  C  E  C  D  H  A
U  B  N  K  O  N  U  C  M  B  C  R  B  E  R
N  I  L  U  V  U  N  D  E  R  T  A  K  E  R
Y  A  T  P  X  T  F  O  B  D  E  G  G  Y  I
V  S  H  B  I  G  B  O  S  S  M  A  N  Q  O
M  E  C  L  E  S  I  H  T  W  T  O  X  Z  R
```

TEXAS TORNADO

He's one of the most popular athletes ever to hail from the great state of Texas. He's a phenomenal second-generation wrestler who possesses a physique that appears to be carved from granite. He's also a former Intercontinental titleholder. He is the Texas Tornado, and he definitely ranks as one of the true superstars in the WWF.

In the ring, the Tornado storms into his opponents and levels them with a collection of suplexes and body-slams. Then, when he senses that conditions are right, the Tornado bounces off the ropes and cuts down the competition with the world-renowned spinning tornado punch. For the opponent, that's the end.

LEGION OF DOOM

Legion of Doom, Hawk and Animal, is the team to beat in the World Wrestling Federation for many reasons. First of all, they are championship material and on any given day have the strength and ring smarts to overcome the biggest and best duos operating in the WWF tag team division. Furthermore, Hawk and Animal have established a successful track record. They have derailed the Orient Express, outdone Power and Glory and virtually ruined every other duo that has

come their way.

Every team that has fallen to the LOD has been hit by their finishing maneuver, the dreaded Doomsday Device. This is the Legion of Doom's signature tactic in which Hawk mounts the top turnbuckles and clotheslines an opponent off Animal's shoulders. Thus far, the Doomsday Device has spelled just that for a bevy of WWF tandems and will probably yield similar results with opponents in future bouts.

CROSSWORD

ACROSS

1 The WWF's reigning champion, he's pictured (5)
8 Earthquake is a Natural_____ (8)
9 Defeats (5)
10 The Bushwhackers like to eat them right out of can (8)
11 The Undertaker's favorite color (5)
14 Enrage (5)
15 The WWF's "Doctor of Style" (5)
20 Clenched hands (5)
21 He's "the excellence of execution" (4,4)

22 Deadly (5)
23 The WWF's Thanks-giving night tradition is known as the _____ *Series* (8)
24 The Million Dollar Man ____ ____Biase (3,2)

DOWN

2 Mean Gene (8)
3 Assaulted (8)
4 Sgt. Slaughter is the Hulk's main one (5)
5 First name of the Macho Man (5)

6 Knocks out (5)
7 Smash's new tag team partner (5)
12 _____ Warrior (8)
13 Rowdy Roddy Piper's homeland (8)
16 Extremely fat, like Earthquake (5)
17 A Nasty Boy, _____ Sags (5)
18 Sgt. Slaughter cracked one across the Hulk-ster's back at *Wrestle-Mania VII* (5)
19 Mistake (5)

THE ROCKERS

Marty Jannetty and Shawn Michaels, who are universally known as the Rockers, say that they both have their eyes on many WWF tag teams.

"That's right, the Rockers are rockin' and rollin', and we don't plan to stop," says Shawn. "There are lots of teams in the World Wrestling Federation. Guys like Power and Glory, the Nasty Boys and the Beverly Brothers are all tough. But they will all go down, just like all the rest, when they meet the Rockers—the Masters of Motion."

ROWDY RODDY PIPER

It seems as if everywhere you look these days you will see Rowdy Roddy Piper. You can see him every week on *WWF Superstars of Wrestling*, where he provides insightful color commentary; you can read about him and see exclusive photographs of his career in the last issue of *WWF Wrestling Spotlight*, a magazine, by the way, that Hot Rod thoroughly loved; or you can see him in action between the ropes.

Currently, Hot Rod is at odds with Irwin R. Schy-

ster, who is otherwise known as IRS. Apparently, Mr. Schyster has told some of his friends at the Internal Revenue Service to look into Piper's finances. Schyster claims Piper has been cheating on his taxes for years, and now, so Schyster says, it's time for IRS to collect. According to the Rowdy One, however, it will IRS who will collecting something. He will collect, says Hot Rod, a bunch of black and blues after the Scotsman finishes with him.

MACHO MAN RANDY SAVAGE

Earlier this summer, Macho Man Randy Savage popped the question to his long-time manager and first love, Miss Elizabeth. Before a worldwide television audience, Savage asked Elizabeth if she would take his hand in Macho matrimony. She accepted, and the two were scheduled to be married at *SummerSlam*.

"Oh yeah," says Savage, "Macho Man and the lovely Elizabeth are going to get hitched and spend the rest of their lives together in Macho matrimony. It's a marriage made in heaven."

PUZZLE ANSWERS

WWF TRIVIA

HOMEBOYS, Glasgow, Scotland, New Zealand and California; **BRAINS BEHIND THE BRAWN**, Jimmy Hart, Slick, Bobby "The Brain" Heenan; **TOUGH TALK**, a price, the Rockers, and Big Boss Man; **HISTORY IN THE MAKING**, Elizabeth, both men were blindfolded, and *WrestleMania 2*; **PHYSICAL ASSETS**, Hulk Hogan, 460 pounds, and the Ultimate Warrior.

How did your wrestling knowledge stack up?

CROSSWORD

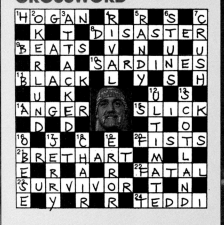

¹H	²O	³G	A	N		⁴R		⁵R		⁶S	⁷C
	K		T		⁸D	I	S	A	S	T	E	R
⁹B	E	A	T	S		V		N		U	
	R		R		¹⁰S	A	R	D	I	N	E	S
¹¹B	L	A	C	K		L		Y		S	H
	U		K						¹²O	¹³D
¹⁴A	N	G	E	R			¹⁵S	L	I	C	K
	D		D						T	O
¹⁶O	¹⁷V	¹⁸C	E		¹⁹E	²⁰F	I	S	T	S
²¹B	R	E	T	H	A	R	T		M	L
E	R	A	R	A	R	²²F	A	T	A	L
²³S	U	R	V	I	V	O	R	T	N	
E	Y	R	R	R	²⁴T	E	D	D	I	

WORD FIND

V	I	R	G	I	L	O	Y	B	N	Q	F	X	U	U
E	S	P	L	E	G	R	O	C	K	E	R	S	Q	L
C	V	B	U	O	H	X	R	M	L	T	B	E	W	T
S	L	I	C	K	U	D	S	E	V	M	T	W	O	I
G	D	S	P	E	L	U	Z	A	T	R	L	A	C	M
C	T	B	V	O	K	Z	I	Q	T	P	X	R	W	A
A	E	A	R	T	H	Q	U	A	K	E	S	L	C	T
M	D	V	X	Y	O	A	B	G	I	R	U	O	F	E
K	D	N	H	R	G	C	K	U	H	F	P	R	X	W
B	I	R	A	U	A	H	T	Y	C	E	C	D	H	A
U	B	N	K	O	N	U	C	M	B	C	R	B	E	R
N	I	L	U	V	U	N	D	E	R	T	A	K	E	R
Y	A	I	P	X	T	F	O	B	D	E	G	G	Y	I
V	S	H	B	I	G	B	O	S	S	M	A	N	Q	O
M	E	C	L	E	S	I	H	T	W	T	O	X	Z	R

Hulk has been Champion **THREE** times.

THE RIGHT MOVES

Legion of Doom: Doomsday Device
Jim Duggan: Running Clothesline
Warlord: Full Nelson
Greg Valentine: Figure-Four Leglock
Jimmy Snuka: Splash from Top Turnbuckle
The Mountie: Carotid Control Technique
Earthquake: Vertical Splash
Big Boss Man: Spike Slam
British Bulldog: Running Powerslam
Haku: Rear Kick
Texas Tornado: The Claw
Ted DiBiase: Sleeperhold

The WWF Has Many Faces

The World Wrestling Federation is based upon the superstars who use daring athleticism to contest the laurels of the ring. Still, there is more to the WWF. The WWF brings the excitement of the squared circle to everyone in the form of publications and merchandise. Wearing apparel. Gym bags. You name it. The WWF supplies it.

WWF wearing apparel, including T-shirts emblazoned with the likenesses of WWF stars, are worn by people around the globe. You'll never know where you will see someone with a Hulk Hogan or Ultimate Warrior T-shirt. Kenya. Singapore. Rome. London. Fans of WWF stars are everywhere.

The WWF presents more than 1,000 live events annually throughout North America and yet more

From teddy bears to the marvels of TV, the WWF ensures that all of its products are of the highest quality.

around the globe. WWF wrestlers appear in rings as distant from one another as Belfast and Tokyo.

To bring WWF action to people across the world, the WWF has television production facilities that are state-of-the-art. WWF television is taped in seven

languages and distributed in more than 40 countries.

WWF stars also appear in motion picture films. WWF Champion Hulk Hogan, for instance, starred in the action film *No Holds Barred* and now headlines the New Line Cinema film *Suburban Commando.* Rowdy Roddy Piper has appeared and starred in several films, including the science fiction thriller *They Live.* Andre the Giant was featured in the romantic adventure *The Princess Bride.*

The WWF also has a publishing division that puts WWF action into print. There are numerous publications, including a monthly magazine with international distribution. There is a monthly program, enabling you to follow the action in the ring at your local arena. Each major WWF pay-per-view television event has its own program, too. Individual WWF stars are spotlighted in a WWF quarterly, and there are an increasing number of special publications, such as the one you are now reading.

The WWF is truly multi-media and multinational. And you are part of it.

WWF WRESTLING

SPOTLIGHT

Volume No. 12

HOT ROD!

Rowdy Roddy Piper

WWF Magazine

OFFICIAL PUBLICATION OF THE WORLD WRESTLING FEDERATION

April 1991

IN THIS ISSUE: WRESTLEMANIA VII

HULK HOGAN
☆☆☆☆☆☆☆☆☆
DEFENDER OF THE FAITH, THE FLAG & HONOR

WWF HULK HOGAN PYTHON POWER

$2.50 U.S. $3.25 Canada £1.65 U.K.

BRUTUS "THE BARBER" BEEFCAKE

Last year at this time, the Barber was still recovering from his tragic parasailing accident, which resulted in severe trauma to his face and skull. Beefcake has since returned to the WWF, opened *The Barber Shop* on *WWF Wrestling Challenge* and has upgraded his massive physique with a specialized training and tanning regimen. "I'll forever be grateful to my fans for their support and get-well wishes," says the Barber. "Without them, I wouldn't have made it back."